HOW TO FIND A JOB IN

SINGAPORE?

Finding a Job,
Guide to Visa Process,
Average Expenses, Taxes &
Salaries in Singapore

By

Rajesh Laskary

Edited by - Anurag Kushwaha

Cover Photograph: Venkata Ramana Gali

Designer - Richa Bargotra

Author - Rajesh Laskary

DISCLAIMER

DEDICATED TO

'You, Papa!'

It was my father who always wanted to see me in Singapore.

We would often sit on the terrace of our home in my town and dream about a prosperous life, free from loans & debts, buying a big house, a huge car and what not. Like a good son, I always wanted to give him the best in life I could because I had seen him struggle throughout his life so that he could give the best Struggling children.

I worked hard (rather desperately) for 4-5 years and paid off all debts, and started a business. It seemed like things were settling but soon time changed and I made huge losses in business and went almost bankrupt. I knew only one way to pay back those debts and that was to 'earn big'. I started trying real hard to go abroad and I did whatever I could.

Today, I do not have anything to give back to him as our dreams shattered just after 10 days of my arrival in Singapore when I heard the news of him meeting an accident. I immediately flew back home and found nothing but emptiness.

It's been more than seven years now. I have been living in Singapore with my wonderful wife, who has always supported me throughout my life and two lovely sons (12 years and 2 years old), hoping he is watching us.

This is not just a book for me but a tribute to my father. I have tried my best to put down everything in writing based on my experience and help fulfil countless such dreams that my father and I were a part of once.

TABLE OF CONTENTS

Preface ix

What is My Story and Why Did I Write This Book?......................... xi

About the Author.. xv

Part 1: Finding a Job in Singapore 1

Chapter 1: Why Singapore?... 3

Chapter 2: Permanent, Contract and
            Short Term Contract Jobs...................................... 9

Chapter 3: The Typical Job Sectors to Apply 12

Chapter 4: Can I Study and Work? How Much Can I Earn? 14

Chapter 5: The Process of Getting a Job and Relevant Visa....... 18

Chapter 6: Important Things to Do Before You Apply
            for Any Job in Singapore.................................... 20

Chapter 7: Preparing for Interviews 36

Chapter 8: Recruitment Consultancies in Singapore................. 40

Part 2: Visa Issues & Precautions... 51

Chapter 9: Visa Issues & Precautions.................................... 53

Chapter 10: What Happens and What to Do If You
             Lose Your Job? 56

Part 3: Average Expenses, Taxes & Salaries........................... 61

Chapter 11: Average Expenses and Taxes................................ 63

Chapter 12: Average Salary in Singapore 69

Chapter 13: Negotiating Benefits and Relocating...................... 72

Chapter 14: Dos and Don'ts in Singapore 75

Afterword.. 77

PREFACE

hough Singapore is a small city island country, have a limited population and natural resources, but it has plenty of opportunities for the right people with the right skill sets. Train yourself hard every day as knowledge and experience are the keys to unlock a multi-key lock of success.

While you're in your native country applying for various jobs and looking for new opportunities in Singapore or elsewhere in the world, this is the time to work hard on your communication skills and English language abilities (if you're not a native English speaker) as English is the main language of communication among people in Singapore. Average Singaporean can have a conversation in English and it is the language that binds people from all over the world who come here.

Understand that your resume can only help you get a call for an interview; from there onwards it's entirely up to you to make it or lose it. Work hard on your technical skills, no matter if you are a cook, developer, tester, business analyst, project manager, an elecrical or mechanical engineer, designer or engaged in any other profession. Only people who are best in their domain are chosen.

Go for advanced training, courses, industry's best certifications, do mock interviews often, do whatever you can to improve your job profile each day. Think as if you have an interview next month and you do not want to lose it. Create a notebook where you take notes of research you have done, interview questions and answers you think should be appropriate, do everything you find suitable to present the best of yourself.

WHAT IS MY STORY AND WHY DID I WRITE THIS BOOK?

I am an Information Security Manager with 15+ years of work experience with some of the best companies in the world like Hewitt, RBS (The Royal Bank of Scotland), JP Morgan & Chase, Credit Suisse, Barclays Capital, Standard Chartered Bank etc.

I have been working & living in Singapore for the last 7-8 years now. I have worked both as a Contract employee and a Permanent employee in Singapore, also with three job consultancies and directly on a company's payroll as well.

Not just this, I have also lost my job twice in Singapore and have managed to get another one.

I have taken many interviews in Singapore and have also appeared for many during the last 7-8 years, while also extensively searching jobs to come to Singapore while I was back in India.

So what is My Story?

In last few years I have been a public speaker at some of the world's most prestigious educational institutions, invited to international conferences besides being a successful cybersecurity professional, I am also the Vice-President to one of the most reputed Non for profit organisation in Singapore.

But before all that I've been through numerous failures, business losses, interview rejections, losing my job multiple times and especially when I needed it most. So here I am with what I have learnt so far in the journey while trying hard to get a job in Singapore while I was back there in India.

Just in order to sell my book I do not promise (and no one can), that by reading this book you'll certainly get a job here but what I can say is this will certainly give you some extra information and guide you to techniques that you can use in your job search based on my own experience.

After reading the book, you will be able to make use of the opportunities available in Singapore. There are several Questions that I have answered in this book like, How to apply for jobs in Singapore and prepare yourself for them? Where to look for resources? Visas and where to get additional information regarding them? You also get a list of 100+ recruitment consultancies and major companies in Singapore that are going to be very helpful for applying jobs here in Singapore.

Be sure there will be disappointments and failures but despite of them all, what you need in addition to this book is strong determination, will power and perseverance until you reach your ultimate goal and I sincerely hope that one day you most certainly do achieve it.

My Two Cents to *Students*, *Professionals* and *Dependents*:

If you are a *Student*:

- Start building your profile from today, go for trainings, certifications while pursuing your graduation/post-graduation.

- Follow the steps mentioned in the book and try hard to get some internship in any of the companies in Singapore.

If you are a *Professional*:

- You have got everything in the book to start with, so do not wait.

- Do not just apply and wait for an interview call. Prepare yourself well so that you do not miss an opportunity if you get a call.

- There is no point in appearing for interviews and not being able to grab the right opportunity you are looking for.

If you are a *Dependent in Singapore*:

- The book will be worth reading and re-reading for you if you are already in Singapore on Dependent Pass.

- Try to find out some references from your spouse's professional and friend circle from the day you are in Singapore.

- Start today as it is going to take you time to get what you are looking for, no matter whether you are actively seeking for work or want to take a break first, and then start.

- Approach to recruiters directly by emailing them, calling them or sending a message on LinkedIn.

- Meet them and discuss your status, skill-set, availability and qualifications to let them know more about you and why you are looking for work.

What is *not* covered in the book?

- Please understand that this is not a comprehensive guide and it does not guarantee a job in Singapore.

- It should only be used as an added handbook or help/tool in your search for a job to find most of the relevant information at one place.

The book is *not* for:

- Those who think that one day some good opportunity will knock their door.

The book is *for*:

- Those who 'believe' in giving their best, work hard until they succeed.

- Those who 'believe' in going a step ahead and grabbing the opportunity, before it knocks someone else's door.

- Those who are determined and persistent in their efforts till they reach their goal.

ABOUT THE AUTHOR

Currently based in Singapore for last 7-8 years, Rajesh Laskary is a *Cybersecurity Professional*, a *Writer & Blogger*, an *International Public Speaker* who has presented himself on various Cyber security subjects in international conferences and at some of the world's best Universities in Singapore, Malaysia, India and Indonesia.

He is also an amateur mountaineer who has climbed Mt. Kinabalu (Malaysia) and Mt. Rinjani (Indonesia) and also has a few half and full marathons under his kitty.

He is the Vice-President of one of the Singapore based Not-For-Profit Organization, working for the development and social engagement of youth and supporting other charities.

He is a passionate blogger who likes to explain things in the simplest ways possible via his blog **www.MyCyberPizza.com**, from time to time and shares his learning and his life experiences with young professionals and students. He also helps those who seek any guidance in life or career choices.

Professional Life:

He holds a PGDBM, B.E.(Hons.) and a Polytechnic Diploma in Computer Science & Engineering. Besides his academics, he also holds some of the world's most prestigious Cybersecurity certifications like CISSP, CISM, CEH, ISO 27001 Lead Auditor, ISO27005 Risk Manager and Certified COBIT5 Implementer, PMP, ACP, PRINCE2 and ITIL, etc.

He started his career as a part time trainer in 2004 and then worked as an Asst. Professor but soon stepped in the corporate world where he was fortunate to work with some of the world's top banks and companies including but not limited to Standard Chartered Bank, Barclays Capital, Credit Suisse, JP Morgan & Chase, Royal Bank of Scotland, Hewitt Associates.

He is also a professional artist in modern and contemporary art and has organised exhibitions for charities and fund raising.

Linkedin: *https://www.linkedin.com/in/rajeshlaskary/*

Blog: *https://www.MyCyberPizza.com*

PART 1

❧

Finding a Job in Singapore

CHAPTER 1

━◡

Why Singapore?

Benefits of Being in Singapore:

- Financial hub of Asia
- A truly international exposure
- Multiracial & multicultural
- Safe & secure
- Low taxes
- Excellent education system
- Viable public transportation

Financial Hub of Asia:

Singapore is one of the 'Best Country To Live' in the world per many international surveys.

Singapore is also one of the top financial centres of the world.

It has world-class infrastructure and also ranks top in ease of doing business index by various global surveys.

A Truly International Exposure:

Singapore is Asia's largest centre for foreign exchange and commodity trading.

Because of the strategic location, Singapore enjoys in Asia, all the world's top banks and multinational companies have its regional headquarters of the Asia Pacific region in Singapore.

Hence there is always a need for talented and skilled people.

Multiracial & Multicultural:

There are a few facts that prove why Singapore is one of the most liveable cities in the word.

- Singapore has never had any racial riots in 50 years of their post independent history.

- Singapore is home to people from various cultural, ethnic, religious backgrounds living in harmony together.

- There are many places in Singapore where you will find a Hindu & a Chinese temple in one premise, with people worshipping together.

- Most of the Singaporeans can speak in English.

- Singapore is also a quite religiously diverse country where people from all walks of life live peacefully.

Safe & Secure:

Safety and security of citizens and residents have been of utmost priority for the government here.

- Singapore is also considered one of the safest countries in the world.

- It's completely safe to experience the nightlife here as the crime rates are quite low.

- Every bus interchange(bus stop), metro station & all the buildings in Singapore is fitted with CCTV surveillance systems.

- Singapore is also one of the most advanced nations in the field of Cybersecurity.

Low Taxes, Excellent Education System & Public Transportation:

Singapore has low tax rates, excellent education system & public transportation which I have tried to cover in different parts of this book.

CHAPTER 2

⌒

Permanent, Contract and Short Term Contract Jobs

What are Permanent, Contract and Short Term Contract Job opportunities in Singapore?

Based on offered job stability, perks or benefits and contract terms we can broadly classify the types of jobs in the Singapore market as follows:

- Permanent Job
- Contract Job
- Short Term Contracts

Permanent Job:

A permanent job means you will be having a job unless you resign or the company terminates you (because they plan to

Shut down or shift the business unit, non-performance or wilful misconduct etc.)

- 'Generally' stable & have long notice period (2-3 months) on either side

- Base salary less but have good bonuses

- Insurance:

  ❑ Medical insurance for self and family

  ❑ Dental insurance (maybe)

  ❑ Good coverage, out patient + Free GP (General Practitioners)

- Leaves:

  ❑ 24-30 annual leaves

  ❑ 14 sick leaves

  ❑ 2 child care leave

  ❑ 1-2 volunteering leave

Contract Job:

A contract job is the one where a recruitment consultancy or agency hires you (you will be an employee of that consultancy, they will be the one signing the agreement with you, they will be the one paying your monthly salaries etc.), and you will be working for some other company as a contract staff.

A contract job in contrary to a permanent job means you will have a job for a specified contract period in your offer letter (e.g. 6-months renewable, 12-months renewable).

If your contract is a 12-months 'renewable' contract, that might get renewed after a specified period or not depending on various conditions.

But generally if in case your contract is not renewed, your recruitment consultancy will try to find another job elsewhere in Singapore, and you also get the time of 1-2 months of your notice period to look for another job.

But a contract job can also be terminated if you resign or the company terminates you (because they plan to shut down the business unit, non-performance or wilful misconduct etc.)

But if you resign, in addition to serving your agreed notice period, you may have to pay back the company 1-2 months of salary and other expenses company incurred in hiring you (hiring process, visa cost etc.) and helped in relocation (the airfare, shipment of your household items etc.)

- 'Generally' 12 months renewable contract
- Have a short notice period (mostly one month) on either side
- Fixed monthly salary (No bonuses or 1-month salary)
- Insurance:
  - Medical insurance for self and but generally not for family
  - No dental insurance
  - Not so good coverage
  - No or very less outpatient coverage
  - Generally SGD5 co-pay for GP
- Leaves:
  - 12-14 annual leaves
  - 14 sick leaves

Short Term Contracts:

A short term contract is for short term assignments, and as soon as the job gets done, it will be over.

A short term contract means it could be only for 3 or 6 months and might not get renewed.

It could specifically be helpful when you are already working in Singapore but have lost your permanent job, or your contract job's contract was not renewed, and you are looking for another job and do not have an offer in hand so far.

This might give you an opportunity to still stay in Singapore for another 3-6 months and look for another permanent or longer contract job.

- 'Generally' 3-6 months non-renewable/renewable contract

- Fixed monthly salary (No bonuses)

- Insurance:

  - Generally no medical insurance (may or may not)

  - No dental insurance

  - Not so good coverage

  - No outpatient coverage

- Leaves:

  - No annual leaves (or can be negotiated)

  - Prorated sick leaves

CHAPTER 3

⌐⌐

The Typical Job Sectors to Apply

The Typical Job Sectors to Apply in:

- Technology:
- UI-UX designer
- Java
- Test Automation
- Python
- Data Science, AI & ML
- Financial Technology Developers
- Cyber security:
  - Pen Testers
  - CyberArk Consultant

- ❑ SailPoint Consultant

- ❑ OIM Developer

- Cloud Technologies:

- AWS, Azure, Google Cloud Engineers

- Cloud Security

- Physicians or General Practitioners

- Linux Administrator

- Hospitality & Service Industry

- HR/Recruitment/Talent Management

- Forex Brokers

- Market Research

- Banking & Financial Services

- Digital Marketing Management

- Supply Chain and Procurement

- Semiconductor, Medical Device Manufacturing

- Consumer Electronics and Manufacturing

- Quality Assurance & Control

- Digital/Marketing Professionals

- Civil & Infrastucture

- Life Science & Healthcare

CHAPTER 4

⌒

Can I Study and Work? How Much Can I Earn?

S o the good news is, if you are studying in Singapore on a student visa, you are eligible to work if you meet certain requirements mentioned below and you do not need to apply for a separate visa for that.

You must be a student of a full-time course of a recognized educational institution. Let's see in detail what are various courses available apart from BTech, MS, MBA, PhD etc.

Student Pass:

If a foreigner has been selected by an "approved educational institution" to pursue a "full-time" course in Singapore, he will need to apply for a Student's Pass.

It's not just for the high end courses like B.E., B.Tech., MBA, MS, PhD etc. which cost more than $50,000 - $60,000 (depending on the college) but you can also go for some courses which would just cost anywhere around $8000 onwards and earn while you learn like:

- Diploma Level Courses Specific to the Industry

- Diploma in Hospitality Management

- Diploma in Tourism And Hospitality

- Diploma in Bakery/Baking

- Diploma in Information Technology

- Diploma in Travel And Tourism,

- Diploma In Entrepreneurship

- MICE & Events and Attractions Industry.

It is always advisable to verify the following information on the respective department's official government website:

1. Check for all the visa/pass related information like type of visa, eligibility etc.

2. Verify the name of educational institute you are applying for on a government website

3. Verify the validity of the course, future job prospects, fees etc.

How much can you earn?

It will certainly depend on your academic profile, your knowledge of the subject, what type of course you're in and whether you're doing a part-time job along with your studies or doing an internship.

For some courses like Diploma In Hospitality Management, Diploma In Bakery/Baking (where the entire course fee is $8000-$12000+).

If you pursue an internship (which could be anywhere from 6 months to 12 months depending on the course), you can get anything above $2300+. This amount is pretty decent in Singapore for a student to survive and possibly save some money on the side as well.

For other courses like Engineering, MBA, MS, etc. if you're on internship, you can earn even higher starting from as low as $2500-$4500 (and sometimes even more than that).

My personal opinion is, if you're thinking for the long-term, you should not focus on money at this point rather take it as an opportunity to get work experience in Singapore (which is regarded very high in any industry you work in, Singapore

This experience will also give you some time and opportunity of on the job learning, professional development, develop the required skill-sets and build a network which will help you in getting a job.

Certification, Training and Tools:

You have two choices here:

1. Get into a debate of:

   - Whether certifications are good or bad?

   - Whether it adds value in your career or knowledge or not?

   - Whether it will help to get you a job or not?

   - Whether you will get an ROI or not on the money spent?

2. Go for a few certifications:

   - Do some research around available certifications in your industry.

- Find the best one.

- Go for it, no matter how hard it is (your hard work of 4-6 months will pay you throughout your life)

Going through Agents:

You must be extremely careful about selecting an agent to help you get the course admission or help with visa formalities.

Mostly, the educational institute will have the agents listed on their website, who can assist you and help provide you all the information required for you to make an informed decision and to help prepare for your enrolment in the college.

The agents would charge you a fee for the help and information provided and a less troublesome experience.

Sometimes if you are applying by yourself, you can always request the college to lessen your college fee (especially it makes sense if the amount you are saving is in a few thousand dollars).

CHAPTER 5

⌒

The Process of Getting a Job and Relevant Visa

The Process of Getting a Job and Relevant Visa?

The best part of getting a job in Singapore is that you do not have to apply for a visa personally. The company or the recruitment consultancy who is hiring you will ask for scanned copies of all your certificates, degrees, diplomas, passport, etc. and will file the visa with respective government department on your behalf.

Here are the steps:

STEP-1: You apply for many job vacancies

STEP-2: For one of the job positions, your profile gets shortlisted

STEP-3: You get an interview call from the HR manager/ Recruitment consultant

STEP-4: The hiring manager schedules a telephonic/Skype interview

STEP-5: If you are selected there could be a couple of more rounds of interviews

STEP-6: You get selected in the interview process

STEP-7: You receive a job offer

STEP-8: You go through negotiations, discussions and accept the offer

STEP-9: The hiring company (or the job consultancy) files visa application on your behalf

STEP-10: If the visa application is successful, your temporary visit pass is issued

STEP-11: You travel to Singapore & join the company on a given date

STEP-12: Your employer schedules an appointment for you /your family with respective government department

STEP-13: You visit the visa office for remaining visa formalities (photo taking, fingerprint scanning etc.)

STEP-14: You get your visa card (physical card) in the next 2-3 weeks

STEP 15: You can continue to work until your pass is valid (generally for 1 or 2 years) & before 2-3 months of expiry of your pass, your employer will apply for the respective pass renewal

(For more information regarding guide to visa process and eligibility requirements etc. you are always advised to refer to respective official government website and not to rely on individual personal information or any agent)

CHAPTER 6

*

Important Things to Do Before You Apply for Any Job in Singapore

- Polish Your Resume

- Build and Use a Cover Letter

- Use LinkedIn to Get a Job in Singapore

- Create Your Job Portal Profile

How to Polish Your Resume?

There are plenty of resources available online including websites, blogs, LinkedIn articles on how your resume or curriculum vitae should look like and I would not like to repeat the same here but would highlight few things with the context of Singapore.

The first page:

- Remember that it is your first impression.

- Keep it simple, yet informative.

- Follow the steps mentioned below-

Resume Keywords:

- Focus on keywords in the job description as well as your resume and ensure that both matches and is tailored as per the hiring manager's needs.

- Concise details of your core skill sets, qualifications & experience.

- Highlight your achievements, certifications, etc.

Number of pages:

- Total 2 or 3 pages should be enough.

- But if you have 20+ years of work experience, then it is justified if you keep it 4-5 pages long.

- Strictly avoid any spelling or grammatical mistakes as people in Singapore are very particular about quality and content.

Updating the resume timely:

Keep an up-to-date copy of your resume with a cover letter ready all the time in your mobile device. Sometimes you might be in office and a consultant calls you. He may have to submit few profiles to the hiring manager at earliest. Probably they might not have been able to find a resource in Singapore, and that's why they are looking for a foreigner and are in a rush to fill the position as soon as possible.

Some Additional Tips for Your Resume While You Look for a Job:

Few things that I noticed personally while looking for a job in Singapore are:

- It would be great to have an MS-Word (.doc/.docx) resume because generally, consultants here will update the header of CV with their company name and then will share it with their clients.

- If you are applying for jobs with PDF resume, consider sending it along with your MS-Word resume.

- Create a separate resume if you are looking for internship opportunities in Singapore.

- Try applying separately to start-ups in Singapore requesting for internship opportunities as they are most likely to be looking for interns than the big companies.

- If you are already a dependent of an employee in Singapore and are looking for a job, do mention in resume that you are on a dependent visa in Singapore.

- The very first line in a resume should mention that clearly (that you are here in Singapore on DP and are looking for a job opportunity).

Make Sure You are Tailoring Your Resume According to the Job Application:

- It has been my personal experience and also a major concern that I've heard from my friends who are recruitment consultants here in Singapore which is that people don't mention the keywords as required for the job application.

- It may so happen that you ended up applying for 500-600 jobs available in your area of expertise and yet just received

1-2 interview calls which did not go well either. Another result could be that you probably didn't get any call at all.

- Yes, that is possible, and it might be happening because you are not giving the hiring manager what they actually need.

Consider the Following Scenario:

So here is the thing, you might apply for 100 jobs per week just for the sake of applying:

- Without understanding the job criteria,

- Without understanding the job description,

- Without knowing the required skill sets for the job

OR

You can apply for 2-3 jobs every day by

- Going through job description in details

- Finding out the keywords

- Doing quick research about the company

- Tailoring your resume accordingly

- Making it appealing for a hiring manager.

The right choice to make is in your hands.

How to Build and Use a Cover Letter?

- Have one if you don't already

- Keep it simple yet informative

- Use it with every job you apply for

- Use a cover letter which is customised according to the job you're applying for

How to Use LinkedIn to Get a Job in Singapore?

Personally, LinkedIn has helped me achieve what I am today. From getting a job to getting invitations for international conferences, to being a speaker in the world's top universities and to build a brand.

Create an attractive LinkedIn profile which stands you apart from the crowd.

This is where your industry-recognised certifications, volunteering, public speaking, article writing or blogging, employment achievements etc. are going to help you.

LinkedIn is going to be the most important part of your job search so very carefully curate your LinkedIn profile.

Please do keep in mind, even before your resume reaches to a job consultant or the hiring manager; the recruitment manager can reach out to LinkedIn searching for a suitable candidate.

Here are some tips on how to build your LinkedIn Profile:

Dos & Don'ts of LinkedIn:

- Always keep a 100% complete profile
- Profile Photo:
  - Your profile must have a profile photo
  - It must be a formal and professional looking photo (avoid selfies)

- Profile Description:
  - ❑ Give a short and precise, eye-catching profile description
  - ❑ Hire a freelancer or ask your contacts who are expert in professional writing for help
- Do not exaggerate your achievements
- Experience & Projects:
  - ❑ Highlight your roles & responsibilities
  - ❑ Highlight your job achievements
- Recommendations:
  - ❑ Request your previous line managers
  - ❑ Request a few of the industry experts who know you
- Volunteering:
  - ❑ Yes it does help you stand out from the crowd
  - ❑ Highlight your voluntary initiatives and activities
- Applying for Jobs:
  - ❑ Before applying for a job on LinkedIn, check what percentage of keywords match with your resume
  - ❑ Tailor your resume to match it to 90-100% before you apply
  - ❑ Update your job search settings (preferences) in LinkedIn

Steps to Update Your Job Search Settings (preferences) in LinkedIn:

How To Find A Job In Singapore?

STEP-1: Go to your LinkedIn Profile-> 'Me'-> 'Settings & Privacy'

STEP-2: Go to 'Job seeking preferences'

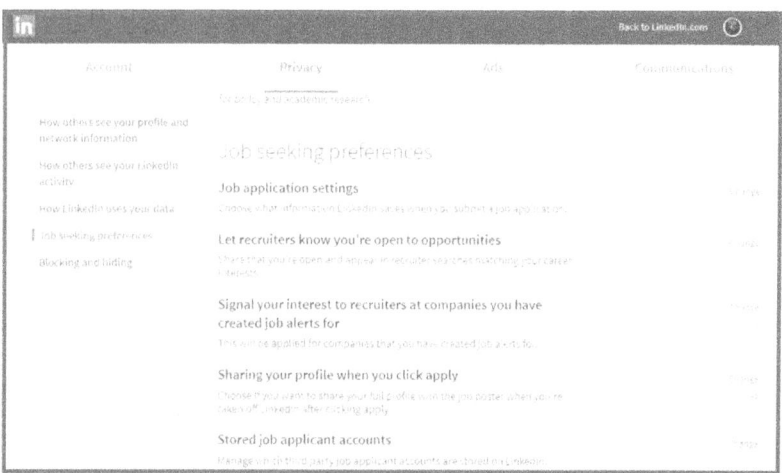

How to Create Your Job Portal Profile?

Please note that most of the global job portals change their location-specific domain name and hence make sure to activate your profile on the local domain of that country and customise it according to the local job market.

E.g.   www.monster.com.sg

         www.jobsDB.com.sg

Some of the things that you need to take care of are:

- Create a full profile on all the major job portals.
- Keep a professional photo in profile.
- Verify & activate your e-mail & mobile number.
- Update your resume timely.
- Have a cover letter attached to the application you make.
- Update 'location' to country where you are looking for a job.
- Provide local references if you know someone who is already working here in Singapore.

Past Job Experiences in Resume:

Sometimes you would like to put all your experience in a resume, thinking it will give more weight to your candidature for the job and would help increase your chances of getting the hiring manager's attention.

Contrary to this, if the resume is too long, it could set a recruiter off. I might sound blunt here, but no one has got time to go through your life history. If the first page cannot impress the hiring manager, there are fewer chances of them giving your application a serious thought. If you're applying for sales and marketing job, your experience while you were a lecturer in a university or college might not be of interest to the recruiter.

- Remove your past experiences which are not relevant to the job.

- Have a LinkedIn URL of your profile in the resume.

- You can still keep your past experiences on LinkedIn; if somebody is interested he can always see it there.

- Make sure your current and past job experiences are consistent in your resume and on LinkedIn or the job portal.

- If you still want to keep it think of how it can help you in the job you are applying for, think what were the common skills between your past job experiences and the job you are applying for and then only keep that relevant information.

Reaching Out to the Network of the Right People:

- In today's world, if you are not making use of professional networking platforms like LinkedIn, you need to give it a serious thought.

- Reach out to the people in your network with a polite and humble message requesting them to let you know if they have a requirement in their organisation.

- You should also ask people to refer you to any of their contact or to some recruitment consultant they know for a particular position. Provide them with a reason for them as why do you feel that you are a good fit for the role.

- Based on my personal experience and having spoken to my recruiter friends here regularly, they have always told me one thing, and that is, they **first** prefer to go to LinkedIn to find out a suitable candidate or to find out some information about the candidate.

- LinkedIn is not the only network to follow. You can reach out to various Facebook groups, LinkedIn groups, Twitter, etc.

- Reach out to any of your friends, former colleagues, former bosses, hiring managers, and relatives anyone you know who is already working in Singapore requesting to refer you for a suitable position you're looking for in Singapore.

- Request your friends, past colleagues, relatives anyone you know is already working in Singapore if they are fine and can allow you to put their name as a reference in your resume (if they are comfortable with it and can give a reference for you when needed).

- Look for the recruitment consultants in your network and approach them with a short and customized message for a job role.

- You can research the job description for which you're planning to apply, find out the keywords, see if that recruitment consultant deals in job requirements of that domain or field and then approach with a well written customised message. Consider the following examples and evaluate yourself, what would you like to receive in a message from potential candidate, if you are the one who is recruiting?

E.g. simply asking 'could you please help me find a job in Singapore?' would not help.

Free Resume Review Websites for Singapore:

There are some free resume review websites in Singapore. You can submit your resume to them for a review, and in a couple of days, they might get back to you with their feedback.

Generally, they may ask you for a nominal fee if you further want a detailed review, design and changes in the resume but it's up to you to decide whether you want to pay for further services, or not.

But if you can get a free review & feedback from 3-4 different websites, you will still have a significant number of points to improve. Some of those websites are:

- www.resumes-central.com

- www.topresume.com

- www.resumebuilder.com.sg

- www.jobscan.co (to scan your resume)

- https://resume.io

Free Cover Letter as per Singapore Job market:

I would highly recommend and encourage you to customise your cover letter as per the Singapore job market before you start applying for jobs here. Your cover letter is the most important part of the process because it reaches to the eyes of the recruiter even before your resume.

It might or might not be read at all depending on how eye-catching it is. Get your cover letter customised as per the local job markets.

There are plenty of free resources available online, and numerous free samples cover letters to download. Spend a few hours and customised or rebuild your cover letter accordingly.

- www.resumeswriter.sg

- www.topresume.com

- www.resumebuilder.com.sg

Job Alerts:

A job alert gives you a 'First Mover' advantage, but you should also be a 'Fast Mover' if you want to be ahead in the race from a crowd of millions. We cannot underestimate the importance of setting up the correct job alert based on your skill-sets, experience and preferences.

Here are a few of them:

Google Alerts:

If you do not know what 'Google Alerts' is, or how to use it, go find out, read and understand and start using it for – job posting alerts, important events in your industry, keeping an eye on employers of your interest.

E-mail Job Alerts from Job Sites:

Enable job alert emails and set a regular frequency & preference of when do you want to receive an email and for what purpose? You might not like to receive several emails every day spamming your mailbox and lose the focus from the ones that are important.

Follow:

Follow the companies; follow the recruiters of the companies you are targeting.

LinkedIn Alerts:

Setup LinkedIn alert for specific companies you are targeting, specific job types (e.g. Full-time, Contract or Part-time etc.), job titles (e.g. Manager, Analyst, and Engineer etc.), location preference (e.g. Singapore), and email or LinkedIn message frequency.

Tell recruiters that you are open to new opportunities – Go to LinkedIn -> Click on "Career Interests" -> Set the setting to on.

Why Your Resume Might Not Get the Hiring Manager's Attention at All:

A typical recruitment consultant or a hiring manager receives hundreds of emails or resume, LinkedIn messages and calls every day. There is something wrong somewhere if you are not getting their attention or if you are not getting the interview calls or email replies. Hiring managers in Singapore are very particular about a few things. They might not give any attention to the best candidate in the queue if there are few things in a resume that they do not expect.

- If your resume is too short or is too long like a book of 5-6 pages

- If the resume is missing the keywords present in the job description

- There are spelling and grammatical mistakes in your cover letter or your resume

- Starting resume with "Objective" statement? Time to change it to the "Summary" section as this will be the first section which draws the attention of hiring manager. Put your experience, achievements and certifications

- Have repeated words or repeated "roles & responsibilities" present in each paragraph or previous job role

- Commenting something negative (maybe a political opinion or on race, religion, etc.) on social media platforms. Think of it and refrain from doing so. World has changed a lot, you are everywhere online and hiring managers are nowadays watching your activities on social media as well before they even think of hiring you

- Your resume is not named properly. Consider the following examples and evaluate what would you like to see yourself?

E.g.

Sample-1: "Resume.doc", "Resume_Rajesh.doc"

OR

Sample-2: "Resume Rajesh Laskary-Singapore.doc" or "Resume_Rajesh Laskary_ Cybersecurity-Singapore.doc."

- If your achievements during a job are not quantifiable. Consider the following examples and evaluate, which resume would you choose having mentioned achievements as below:

E.g.

Sample-1: 'Was responsible for day to day project management and delivered the projects in time and within budget.'

OR

Sample-2: 'Achieved 27% of cost savings by delivering projects before the deadline by using 30% of automation.'

OR

'Helped increase the revenue by 7% as the client started using the application delivered as part of the project three months early.'

Why You Should Not Apply for the Same Job Twice or More With Different Consultants?

Do keep track of your job application. **Do not** apply for the same job twice from different recruiters. Yes, this is very important, and I will explain later why it is so.

1. Apply for a job via the website of the recruitment consultant company.

2. Reach out to the respective recruiters via email, call, LinkedIn message or via the job board itself.

3. Tell them about your job application and why do you think you are a good fit for the role.

4. Wait for their response.

5. In most of the cases, they will reply by saying they will look into it and will update you accordingly.

6. Send a thank you email summarising what you have discussed, and you will be looking forward to their reply.

7. Follow up at the agreed time or as discussed and request for application status.

But, What If You Did Not Receive a Response at All in the Very First Place?

Take a chance and apply via a different consultant company.

Now let me tell you, what happens if you apply for the same job twice or more with different consultants:

Assume that there is a role of 'Java Developer' available with an international bank. There will be many recruitment consulting firms for which the bank is a client and will be paying them a certain commission or fee to help it fill the position.

Those firms will be competing to fill that position and provide the most suitable candidate for the job role. If you applied for a job role first via company A and then also from company B after a few days and suppose, you did not receive a call from company A, and you did not do a follow-up. Now after a few days, someone from company B found your profile suitable and approached you.

The first question generally recruiters ask here is 'Have you applied for this job before?' and if the answer is 'yes', then company B may not decide to take your application forward to the client.

It is because it will be already in their database and the client might not consider you to be company B's candidate, and B does not make any profit out of it.

What Should You Do Then?

1. Be patient and **wait**.

2. Follow the above mentioned seven steps and follow up.

3. Tell company B clearly about your application with A and the current situation and ask if they can help.

4. If you have received a call from B, ask them if they have any similar roles available with them.

5. If not, ask for their email address, send a thank you note and request to keep you in mind and let you know if they come across any relevant job opportunity for you.

6. Follow up after some time, build a relationship.

(Trust me, this has worked for me)

CHAPTER 7

Preparing for Interviews

How to Prepare for Interviews?

It is a very commonly asked, and most generic question asked on all job boards, and I can write an entirely new book on it, and we already have many available. But I'd like to touch on a few things you need to know with the context of Singapore.

Work on interview basics:

- Work on basic interview and communication skills

- Expect and prepare well for a Skype/ WhatsApp video call

- Be attentive to your attire & attitude during the video interview

- Be in a quiet, noise-free environment, with a good internet connection

- Use a good quality microphone

- Test your microphone & speaker (I suggest using a headphone)

- Practice a lot of mock interviews, do a dry run with your friend/family member

What are some of the Most Commonly Asked Interview Questions?

I have added some of the most commonly asked questions during the interviews which might boost your chances of being eligible for the job if answered properly.

Common Interview Questions:

These are the most commonly asked job interview questions in Singapore. Take time to think, do some research, analyse and phrase your answer carefully.

Keep one or two examples ready in mind about every situation/question given below. Note down somewhere the questions and answers in your language if you are not very comfortable in English or are not a native English speaker, or even if you forget easily.

- How did you hear about us?

- Tell us something about your previous experience.

- Why do you want to relocate?

- What do you find interesting about this job?

- What are your strengths and weaknesses?

- How could you be an asset to our company?

- Why should we hire you?

- What are your responsibilities in your current job/company?

- Why do you want to join our company?

- What do you know about our company?

- Please give us an example of a challenging or conflicting situation that you have overcome?

- Can you describe a stressful situation in your last project and how did you deal with it?

- What has been the recent event/news in your area of expertise?

- Why are you leaving your current job?

- What do you like about your job?

- Do you prefer to work independently or as part of a team?

- Where do you see yourself in the next 3-5 years career-wise?

- What was a mistake you made lately?

- Would you mind working for late hours?

- Do you have any questions for us?

How to Answer Interview Questions?

- Be honest

- Keep an answer ready all the time

- Ensure that and be careful, so it does not sound rehearsed

- Do thorough research about the company you are being interviewed for

- At your side, you need to prepare questions for the interviewer as well:

  ❑ Ask about their team structure

  ❑ Ask about projects in the pipeline

  ❑ Ask about the challenges they face

  ❑ What do they expect of you?

  ❑ What are the key technologies they work in?

  ❑ What are the career growth prospects?

CHAPTER 8

~

Recruitment
Consultancies in Singapore

There are many job consultancies or recruitment agencies in Singapore which are popular among candidates seeking for a job opportunity. You can follow below steps to look for them and apply for a job matching your experience, expertise. Create your job account on each of these sites; verify your email address and mobile number.

Yes, it is an arduous and time-consuming process, but this is what will increase your chances of getting an interview call.

Even if you target creating one account on a job site every day and 2-3 job sites every weekend, it should be done in a month or two.

Here are the Main Job Sites Used Among Recruiters in Singapore:

- https://sg.jobsdb.com
- www.eFinancialCareers.com.sg
- www.bestjobs.com.sg
- www.recruit.net
- www.regionup.com
- www.monster.com.sg
- www.JobsCentral.com.sg
- https://gradsingapore.com

  (for fresh graduates)
- www.JobStreet.com.sg
- www.indeed.com.sg
- www.stjobs.sg
- http://sgcareers.com.sg
- www.fastjobs.sg
- https://startupjobs.asia/
- www.cultjobs.com

  (to find creative jobs)
- www.findsgjobs.com
- https://glints.com/sg
- www.mytechlogy.com
- www.topfinancialjobs.com.sg

  (for financial jobs)

Here are Major Recruitment Consultancies to Apply for a Job in Singapore (Not necessarily in any particular order or sequence):

- www.robertwalters.com.sg
- www.roberthalf.com.sg
- www.ambition.com.sg
- www.hays.com.sg
- www.kellyservices.com.sg
- www.randstad.com.sg
- www.dpsearch.com.sg
- www.glassdoor.sg
- www.primestaff.com.sg
- www.nsearchglobal.com
- www.arc-hr.com.sg
- www.michaelpage.com.sg
- www.nityo.com
- www.beacon-search.com
- www.3csynergy.com
- https://achievegroup.asia
- www.evolutionjobs.com/sg
- www.gsiexecutivesearch.com
- www.farorecruitment.com
- www.morganmckinley.com.sg

- www.hudson.sg
- www.garnerintl.com
- www.airswift.com
- www.connectus-group.com
- www.3ipeople.com
- www.itcan.biz
- www.accionlabs.com
- https://singapore.job-q.com
- www.spencerstuart.com
- www.frazerjones.com
- www.recruitexpress.com.sg
- www.u3infotech.com
- www.shellinfotech.com
- www.gatewaysearch.com
- https://aryansolutions.tech
- www.mangotree.com.sg
- www.manpowergroup.com
- www.helius-tech.com
- www.job-applications.com
- www.aegis-recruitment.com.sg
- www.jobline.com.sg
- www.3csynergy.com
- www.kerryconsulting.com

- www.talent-merge.com
- http://comtel-solutions.com
- www.theoptimum.net
- www.hudson.sg
- https://recruitplus.com
- www.jac-recruitment.sg
- www.capitasingapore.com
- https://neuvoo.com
- http://realsoftinc.com
- www.gmprecruit.com
- www.alliancerecruitmentagency.com
- www.jac-recruitment.sg
- www.persolsg.com
- www.rgf-executive.com
- www.gmprecruit.com
- www.ctes.com.sg
- www.scienteinternational.com
- www.ojassociates.com
- www.accionlabs.com
- www.headhunt.com.sg
- www.ridik.net
- https://flintex.com.sg
- www.enggsol.net

- www.searchpersonnel.com.sg

- www.juhlerprofessionals.com.sg

- www.searchnetwork.com.sg

- www.horizon-recruit.com

- www.logisticscareer.sg

- www.evolutionjobs.com/sg/

- www.recruitexpress.com.sg

- www.recruit-inc.com

- www.mcgregor-boyall.com/index-asia

- www.recruitmenthubasia.com

Here are Few Companies Specialised in Their Domain to Apply for:

- www.softenger.com

  (for QA & testing, Singapore office)

- www.gatewaysearch.com

  (recruiting in Accounting, Finance, Tax)

- www.energyresourcing.com

  (for energy and resource industries)

- www.faststream.com

  (specialist in maritime & shipping industry)

- www.adecco.com.sg

  (specialist HR recruitment consultancy)

- www.earthstreamglobal.com

  (for energy & infrastructure)

Applying for Jobs in Major Banks & Financial Services Companies:

Singapore is called the financial hub of Asia, and hence almost all world's top banks and financial institutions have their regional headquarters or offices here in Singapore.

I would advise visiting the 'Career' section of each website, create your account, look for the job matching your criteria, apply and keep a watch on the application status.

If you are doing this, you are significantly increasing your chances of getting an interview call from those job applicants who are not doing this.

The reason is, sometimes most of these companies will publish a job first on their website, and then if they are not able to fill in these positions, they will give it out to recruitment consultancies.

Major Banks & Financial Services Companies are:

- The Development Bank of Singapore (DBS)
- The Post Office Savings Bank (POSB)
- United Overseas Bank (UOB)
- The Overseas-Chinese Banking Corporation (OCBC Bank)
- CIMB Singapore
- Standard Chartered Bank
- J.P. Morgan Singapore
- Morgan Stanley
- Citibank

- Credit Suisse

- Barclays Bank

- Deutsche Bank

- The Royal Bank of Scotland (RBS)

- HSBC

- BNP Paribas Singapore

- Maybank Singapore

- State Bank of India

- Bank of China

- ANZ Singapore

- RHB Bank Singapore

- Singapore Exchange (SGX)

- Bank of America Merrill Lynch

- Visa Worldwide Pte Ltd

- Goldman Sachs

*This list given above is not comprehensive but you can search for all the major banks in Singapore one by one and apply on their website. I have received interview calls from some of the banks of which I had never heard the name before.

You may consider starting to apply for individual bank websites as even though they are banks they always have requirements for HR, Accounting & Audit departments, Marketing, Information Technology, Cyber Security, etc.

- Go to the respective bank's website

- Create your account on the 'Careers' page

- Search for vacancies matching your profile
- Apply and keep a track of the status
- Follow up

Some Additional Things to Do:

- Social media groups – Join some social media groups on Facebook or LinkedIn related to jobs in Singapore.
- Applying directly on company websites.
- Calling and speaking to recruiters directly.
- Building good personal rapport with consultants, recruiters or people you're networking with.
- Be enthusiastic, open to relocate and learn to be polite while you receive the call.
- Networking with your friends, ex-colleagues, ex-managers & others.
- Having the scanned copies of the entire documents ready all the time.

E-mails:

- Reach out instead of waiting for an opportunity to knock your door
- Don't forget to say a "Thank you!" post your interview or a call from the hiring manager.
- Be proactive in replying an E-mail, continuing communication and the follow-ups.

- Be very careful about your grammar and spellings while you send an email.

- Use a signature with your mobile number (and alternate number) and E-mail ID.

- Do not delay in replying e-mails.

PART 2

Visa Issues & Precautions

CHAPTER 9

~~

Visa Issues & Precautions

So, for example, if a company offers you a fixed monthly salary of SGD 5,600 (more experienced candidates need higher salaries) then the company will apply for your relevant visa/pass which could be valid up to 1,2 or 3 years depending on various conditions.

Visa in Singapore:

- All foreigners who intend to work in Singapore must have a valid pass (commonly known as a work visa in Singapore) before they can start to work here.

- There are many guide to visa process available for working professionals based on their salary, experience, skill-set etc.

Similarly Foreign workers who are in the field of construction, manufacturing, marine shipyard etc and are at lower end of salary may be issues different pass.

Every individual is always advised to visit the relevant official government website for detailsed and most accurate information.

However, if you're more experienced and are offered a very high fixed monthly salary, the company may apply for your visa which has greater flexibility longer validity

Be Aware! Be Cautious! Be Safe!

Be aware of any scam all the time while dealing with any agent or middle-man in Singapore or your native country who promises to get you a job in exchange for some money.

Understand that Singapore is very strict about laws, and if you do not satisfy the eligibility criteria for the visa passes, you can't get in.

All government websites here gives you all the necessary information in a very detailed format on all guide to visa process based on your educational qualification, experience, etc.

Go through the kind of pass (visa) category; you would fall in to and follow respective website to understand following carefully:

- Is this visa is for me?
- Can I apply?
- What is the qualifying salary for this type of visa?
- For how long this pass/visa will remain valid?
- Check whether is it renewable?
- Know work visa requirements

- What are the visas issued for the family members?

- Check what documents are needed before applying?

(And several other important points)

Are Your Dependent Eligible to Work in Singapore?

- Know what is the visa for Dependents?

- Understand what is the 'Letter of Consent'?

How to Find a Job in Singapore?

- Prepare your mindset.

- It is not going to happen on the spur-of-the-moment.

- Dedicate some time to job hunting regularly.

- Be patient.

- Make yourself visible.

- Apply on **job portals**.

- Apply to **recruitment consultancies**/agencies.

- Apply for a job on LinkedIn.

- Apply with the help of **your network**.

- Apply on the **company websites**:

  ❑ Banks in Singapore

  ❑ Companies in Singapore

- Create an Excel sheet.

- Keep track of your job applications & follow up.

CHAPTER 10

～

What Happens and What to Do If You Lose Your Job?

hat if you lose your job in Singapore or your contract is not renewed with the company. This could be a nightmare for anyone especially if you are married and have kids. I know the pain as I have gone through it as well.

What Are the Situations you can lose Your Job In?

1. Wilful misconduct, racial abuse, involvement in criminal activities.

2. Breach of contract terms and conditions.

3. The company goes out of business.

4. The company plans to shift the business unit or a department to some other country (low-cost locations generally).

How Does the Process Work Once You've Lost Your Job?

- Generally when you are given a pink-slip, you are given one or two months notice by your consultancy (the company that employs you) depending on your contract and you are told about your **last working day.**

- Now the consultancy will start finding another job and help arrange interviews for you with the same client but in some other department or with any other client of theirs where they may have few vacancies or with some other clients.

- You can also start looking for another job from that day onwards (with any other company too) so that you have high chances of getting a job in case your consultancy is not able to secure a job for you in that time frame.

- On the day of completion of your notice period, your work visa pass will be cancelled. Now you exactly have one more month to stay in Singapore and will have to leave Singapore on or before the 30th day.

- If you manage to clear some interview and get shortlisted for the job, the consultancy will again apply for your work visa for 12 or 24 months (depending on the requirement and many other factors but generally this is the norm), and you can continue to work in Singapore if your visa application is successful.

What can you do?

Let us analyse all of the above one by one:

1. Wilful Misconduct, Racial Abuse, Involvement in Criminal Activities:

   - Singapore has some of the toughest laws and fines. They call it 'Fine City'. So if you are involved in petty issues like smoking out of designated area, spitting on roads/public areas there are CCTV cameras everywhere, and even if it's not there, you never know who is watching you and who will report and you can be fined for few hundred dollars (for first time offenders).

   - But as far as wilful misconduct, racial abuse, involvement in other criminal activities are concerned, rest assured if you are involved in any of above activities there are high chances that you will be fined, charged in a court of law and will be deported immediately.

   - What can you do? So the advice would be to always refrain from any such activities as even a small fine could potentially impact your visa renewal application.

2. Breach of Contract Terms and Conditions:

   - It is an obvious one as in any other country and depends on the contract and its terms and conditions; you have signed with your prospective employer. And hence you may be also likely to lose a job if you have breached any of the contract terms and conditions.

   - What can you do? So the advice would be to always act per the contract.

   - Read the terms and conditions very carefully.

3. The Company Goes out of Business:

   - There are very high chances that the company itself might go out of business or start making losses if it's a start-up and does not have sufficient funds to sustain further challenges.

   - What can you do? Start looking for a new job right then.

4. The Company Plans to Shift the Business Unit or a Department to Some Other Country (Low-Cost Locations Generally):

- Most of the times, this is the main reason companies fire the entire business units or a bunch of employees. Some companies do provide severance packages for its permanent employees but not all do so.

If you are a contract employee, certainly there are no severances packages for you, then what can you do?

1. While all the steps I mentioned above under *'What happens when you lose your job?'* may be taking place, start looking for a new job right now.

2. Save enough (Singapore Dollars) to survive without a salary for a couple of months.

3. Build a network of people while you're here in Singapore.

4. Approach as many of your contacts or LinkedIn contacts as you can.

5. Customise your cover letter; resume as per the job requirements.

6. Approach as many job consultancies as you can.

7. Apply for as many jobs as you can on various job portals and companies.

8. Getting a job is not easy; you have to do what it takes to be at the position you are looking for.

There is no *one* secret of getting a job in Singapore or elsewhere in the world.

It takes hard work, and there are no shortcuts. You cannot afford to do what everyone else is doing; you will have to make extra efforts to stand out from the crowd which others in the same queue are not doing.

This book has many things that you can do, cannot do or avoid but remember one thing, everything you do from improving your resume to set up job alert you are one step ahead of others who have not done so.

If you have set up job alert in LinkedIn or on a job portal, or you have reached out to a recruiter by sending an email or a personal message you are a step ahead from those who have not done so.

PART 3

Average Expenses,
Taxes & Salaries

CHAPTER 11

⌒

Average Expenses and Taxes

Low Taxes:

Singapore has very low or moderate tax rates for individuals. If your salary is less, tax will be very less and if your salary is high then you may have to pay a little bit extra.

Based on the salary you are expecting in Singapore, you should always check with the company about following information. What are the tax benefits in your salary range and how much? What will be your take home salary post tax deduction, focusing on following:

- Tax benefits:
- Tax rebates
- Tax calculator

The Tax Calculator

You may request from the HR or ask them to guide you to relevant official government website to download the tax calculator (this is a very simple Excel sheet) to calculate the taxes as per the minimum salary you expect before you plan to move to Singapore.

- It is straightforward to use Excel Tax calculator.

- Fill in your annual income (which you expect).

- Fill in all the section where you expect a rebate.

- And it will automatically calculate your annual tax liability at the bottom of the sheet.

So for example, You can download an up to an annual salary of SGD 20,000, there might not be any tax on that and the maximum tax may be up to 22% for higher salaries with numerous rebates and incentives.

Average Expenses:

There are mainly two types of residences available in Singapore - an *HDB* and *Condominium.*

An HDB flat is the one constructed by the government and is cheaper than the condominiums (which are constructed by private builders and are a bit expensive than government-owned flats).

HDB Flats are neat and clean and have all basic amenities required including a public garden area, kids play area etc. but do not have facilities like gym, swimming pools, etc.

Please note that all the rents mentioned below are an approximation and change every year slightly. You can refer to sites like 'PropertyGuru' to get a closer estimate of rents in Singapore (which further can be negotiated with house owner or the property agents).

A. For Bachelors:

i. Accommodation

- Sharing a common/master room in HDB or in a Condominium:

  If you share a common room/master room (a master room is a big room having an attached bathroom) in a flat where a family is already living, and you don't mind sharing a room in an already occupied apartment this is for you.

- HDB Flat:

  You can share a common room at a rent of around average 500-700 SGD per month and master bedroom at 800-900 SGD per month.

- Condominium:

  You can share a common room at a rent of around average 700-900 SGD per month and master bedroom at 900-1100 SGD per month.

- Negotiate whether the rent includes PUB (Public Utility Bills – Internet, Electricity, Water etc.) or not, if not how much are you expected to pay?

- If you would like to cook at home, negotiate and confirm in advance with the house owner about your frequency of cooking, types (Veg/Non-veg, etc.).

ii. Food

- Cooking at home:

  Yes this is one of the cheapest options to save your monthly food bill if you love to cook at home. For the price of groceries and for a more accurate approximation you can see the price at Fairprice, Singapore's website and calculate.

- Eating outside in Singapore is like experiencing a heaven of foods, and you will find not just hundreds but thousands of variety of food here. For one person eating a meal outside may cost between SGD 8-9 to SGD 15-20 depending on where and what you are eating.

iii. Commutation

Public buses and MRT (the trains) are the most convenient and cheapest option in Singapore to daily commute between office and work. You may spend approximate SGD 90-150 per month on it.

B. For Family:

i. Accommodation:

- Renting a studio apartment or a 2/3 BHK in HDB and the prices can start from SGD 1600 - 1800 (1BHK), SGD 1600 - 1800 (2BHK), SGD 1900 - 2300 (3BHK).

- Renting a studio apartment or a 2/3 BHK in Condominium and the prices can start from SGD 1600 - 1800 (Studio), SGD 1800 - 2100 (2BHK), SGD 2100 - 2600 (3BHK).

- How can you save 25% of your monthly rent?

   If you don't mind sharing your extra room with a stranger, you can always share a room with someone who can pay you a monthly rent and have a contract for 6 months/12 months per your convenience and agreement with the tenant.

ii. Groceries/Food:

Your monthly groceries may range between SGD 400-500 to SGD 600 and above depending on number of family members and products you buy. But for a more accurate approximation, you can see the price at Fairprice, Singapore's website and calculate.

iii. Commutation:

Public buses and MRT (the trains) are the most convenient and cheapest option in Singapore to daily commute between office and work. You may spend approximate SGD 90-150 per month per person if you commute daily.

iv. Education:

There are two types of schools in Singapore:

1. Local Government Schools

2. International Schools

These few articles available on the internet will give you an idea of the quality of education provided in Singapore.

Education System in Singapore:

Singapore school education tops in global education rankings.

Let's understand the Local and International schools in detail.

Local Government Schools:

Admissions:

It is a little bit tough now to get into the local government schools, and International students who are willing to take admission to the mainstream schools at the Primary 2 to 5 or Secondary 1 to 3 levels must take part in an admission test for international students.

Fees:

Approximate fees for local schools are:

- Primary   : SGD 700+

- Secondary   : SGD 1250+

International Schools:

Admissions:

There are plenty of international schools in Singapore.

Though all international schools may have slightly varying criteria for the admission of the child, generally you have to submit an online admission form, and you are requested to pay the registration fee, once this is done then you are expected to meet the admission counsellor for an assessment test of the child and verification of documents.

Fees:

- Average SGD 2500-3500 Per Month (Depending on schools)

v. Other expenses:

PUB (Public Utilities Bills) may include your electricity and water (which will be around SGD 200+) and Internet, TV (SGD 60-80) and mobile plan (SGD 70-100). For eating outside, you can refer to the above section for per person approximates.

CHAPTER 12

⌒

Average Salary in Singapore

S alaries in Singapore vary greatly like any other country based on the skill sets and experience you have and the current market situation as well. But let us look into some average salary structure and how it works in Singapore:

What Is the Average Salary in Singapore?

Average salaries for 'majority' of the professionals (foreigners) in Singapore range between $4000 and $14000 every month and it depends on many factors as mentioned below

- Number of years of experience

- Niche skills you have experience in

- The urgency of the hiring manager

- Current availability of resources for the required set of skills in the Singapore market

To give you an example and a little bit of perspective consider three developers trying to apply for a job in Singapore:

Developer A:

If a developer is being hired for Java development and has around 5-7 years of work experience in various Java development may get somewhere between SGD 5,500-6,500.

Developer B:

If the developer is working in Fintech and has experience in the development of new financial application tools will help a financial institution in digital transformation and generate more revenue, he may in that case, get SGD 7,000-8.000.

Developer C:

Let us say, a developer is applying for the same job but also has some experience in Block chain technology, or any other latest technologies he even might get somewhere around SGD 8,000-10,000.

Above rule applies to almost any job role in technology space but moreover one or the other similar parameters may decide the salary in all other industries as well.

Where to Check for Average Salaries?

- Mentioned below are few most popular websites and common sources where you can find an approximation of the average salaries for various roles across different industry verticals:

- www.glassdoor.com

- www.payscale.com

- www.salary.sg

- There are also some of the major job consultancies that publish annual/quarterly reports on latest salaries in Singapore across different industry verticals:

- www.morganmckinley.com.sg

- www.michaelpage.com.sg

- www.kellyservices.com.sg

- www.hudson.sg

- www.adecco.com.sg

I am sure after going through above sites for the specific role you are looking for, you will be able to figure out a very close range of the salary you might expect based on your experience and skill sets.

CHAPTER 13

╼

Negotiating Benefits and Relocating

How to Negotiate Salary?

If you have reached this point where you have got your offer letter that means your hard work and perseverance has paid off.

While you are excited to have been offered the job you had dreamt of at the same time you feel that unfortunately, the compensation is not what you were expecting.

So I will leave it to your discretion whether you want to negotiate or not. I did not do it because I was already offered a good salary in comparison to what I was getting at that time in Indian currency. And my main aim was to come to Singapore.

This is the time to negotiate, but you might be scared of losing the job offer if you negotiate further.

Even if you negotiated, but the HR or the hiring manager is reluctant to increase the salary, there is still a room for negotiation on other perks or benefits before you give up. Some of these could be:

- Paid annual leaves
- Sick leaves
- Mid-year appraisals
- Medical insurance for dependents
- Relocation amount
- Relocation benefits
- Any stock or option plan

Remember, a polite discussion or request might work wonder, and there is no harm in asking.

You might not get what you are asking for, but still, a little bit more is always good.

How to Ask for Benefits/Relocation?

- Again it will largely depend on whether you are being hired for a contract job or a permanent one.

- If you are joining on a contract position (short/ long term contract) do not expect much but you can always politely negotiate what is comfortable for you and the company.

Benefits and relocation also depends largely on the nature of the job you are being hired for whether permanent or a contract job.

Benefits/Relocation in a Permanent Job:

- If you are lucky enough and have got a permanent position with a multinational company, there are high chances that they may bear the cost of:

- Your visa application

- One way airfare to you and your immediate family

- Shipment of your household items (in rare cases but it does happen)

- Your hotel stay in Singapore for the initial few weeks

- And if you are even luckier then you might also get some relocation amount

Benefits/Relocation in a Contract Job:

Do not worry if you did not get a permanent position. Singapore is the land of opportunities.

Once you are here and have spent a year or two on a contract position, you may get a permanent position, as well as companies prefer to hire those candidates who are available locally in Singapore.

The job consultancy or the recruitment firm who has applied your visa (your employer) may bear the following costs:

- Your visa application

- Visa application for your family (Dependent Passes)

- One way airfare to you

- One way airfare to your immediate family (Depends on how you negotiate)

- Your hotel stay in Singapore for the initial few weeks

CHAPTER 14

⌒

Dos and Don'ts in Singapore

Dos:

- Be respectful and considerate to others (e.g. in elevators, public transport, people are not comfortable even if your body is touching theirs due to the crowd and rather prefer to avoid the crowded bus/MRT and instead wait for the next one.

- Follow the traffic rules.

- Be in queue - in restaurants, public transport, malls etc.

- Say 'Thank You'. Yes, this is very important, and people can easily get offended if you do not say so.

Don'ts:

- Do not speak negatively about any race or religion.

- Do not spit or throw litter in public places or anywhere in Singapore.

- Do not smoke anywhere except designated smoking zones.

- Do not push or touch anyone if you are on a crowded bus or MRT.

AFTERWORD

S o now you have a good amount of information, you know which portal will give you free samples of cover letters that can be used for applying jobs in Singapore, portals which offer you free reviews and feedback for your resume quality, the top companies and consultants in Singapore where you can apply, but the big question is:

What Do You Do Now?

So here is the step-by-step process which you need to follow. For few it may be just a couple of months, for others it can take months or years. But you will have to be persistent in your efforts. Consider it like running a marathon. Some will be able to run faster, ahead of others, some will complete it but will take some time; some will take way more time (a marathon generally needs to be finished in 6 hours) but will still make it. Some will not be able to make it in their first attempt but will make it the next time.

Don'ts:

- Do not be desperate.

- Do not get disheartened if you do not see any results soon.

- Do not give up.

Dos:

- Continue to apply.

- Continue to build your profile while you are busy applying.

- Go for professional courses which you think can help in your career.

- Go for advanced level training in your field of work.

- Go for industry's best certifications.

- Keep improving yourself.

How Do You Start From Here?

1. Take decisions first, set a goal and stick to it.

2. Invest a few hours in creating a cover letter.

3. Invest a few days to create a resume.

4. Create an Excel sheet where you'll track your progress and application status (E.g. Column name Job Portal/Company, Role, Applied On, Consultant, Email, Mobile number, Status, Comments, etc.)

5. Start doing your research on various available job opportunities – job portals, recruitment firm portals, your network, LinkedIn, etc.

6. Start approaching people for reference.

7. Find out a job role and see what amount of keywords in your resume matches with job description (You can see that in LinkedIn and many another job portals).

8. Customise your cover letter, resume as per job description.

9. Apply on LinkedIn.

10. Apply on Job portals.

11. Apply on the web portal of recruitment firms/job consultancies.

12. Apply on direct company portal.

13. Apply for one to five jobs every day at least based on how occupied you are with your job and other commitments.

14. Take out time to apply for at least 5-10 jobs every weekend.

15. Follow up on your job applications – send emails, call and message on LinkedIn.

16. Keep building the network and establish a relationship.

17. Keep updating your Excel records.

18. If you receive a call from a firm, understand the requirements thoroughly.

19. Be ready to answer questions I have mentioned in the interview section.

20. Keep the discussion relevant to the job description.

21. If you get an offer letter then follow the steps mentioned in the book.

22. Negotiate and make sure you settle for mutual benefits.

23. If the book helps you get a job in Singapore, come and meet me in person when you arrive here (and yes, the coffee is on me).

Best of Luck!

Note: All the amounts mentioned in the book are in Singapore dollars but are just for your reference and example purposes only. Please do your own research and due diligence before taking any decisions.

www.ingramcontent.com/pod-product-compliance
Lightning Source LLC
Chambersburg PA
CBHW051327220526
45468CB00004B/1524